R. M. Rayner

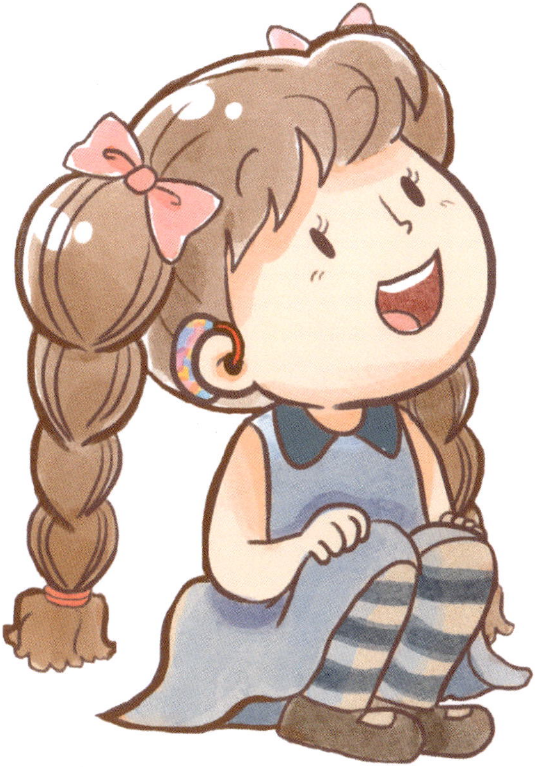

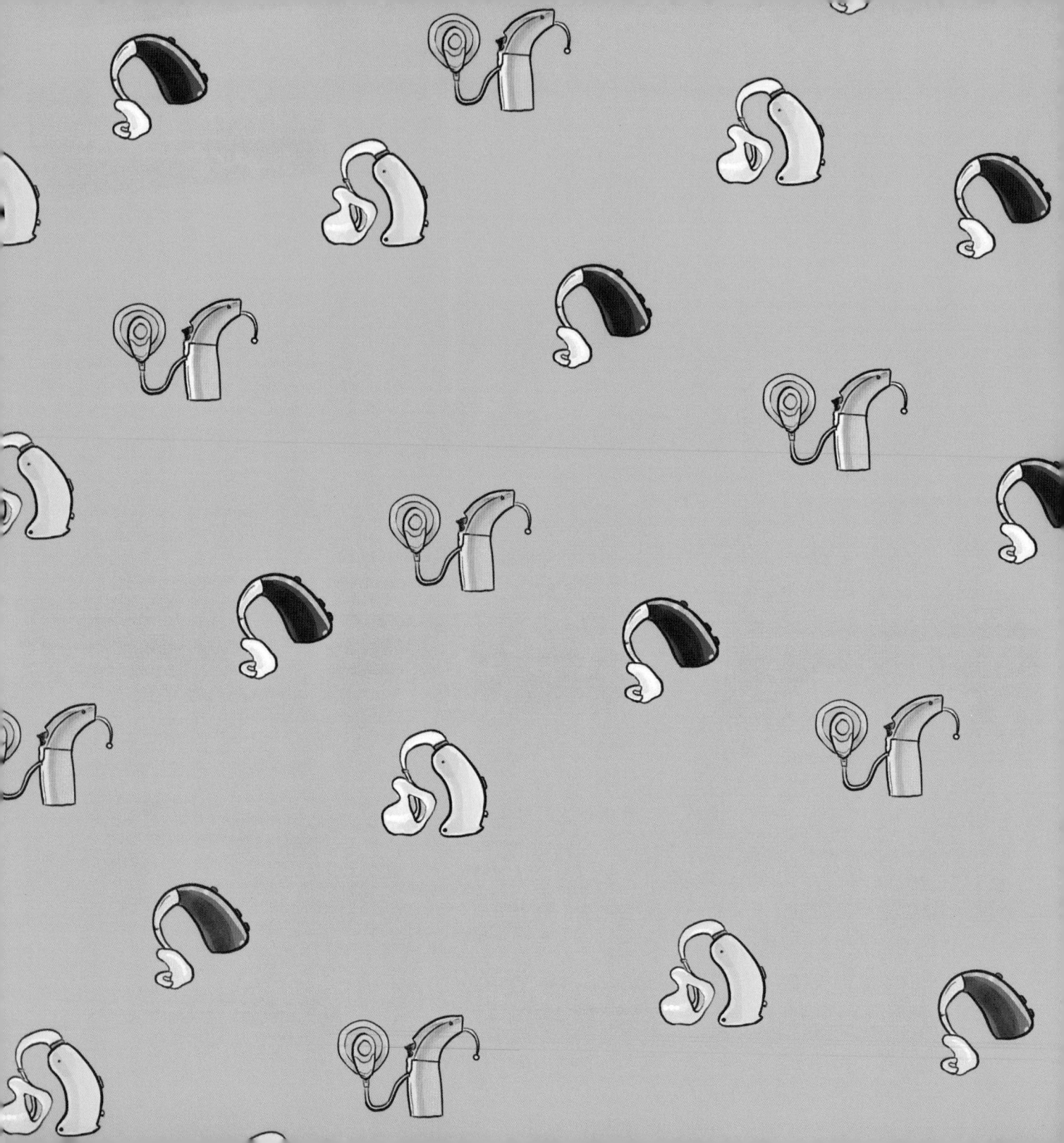

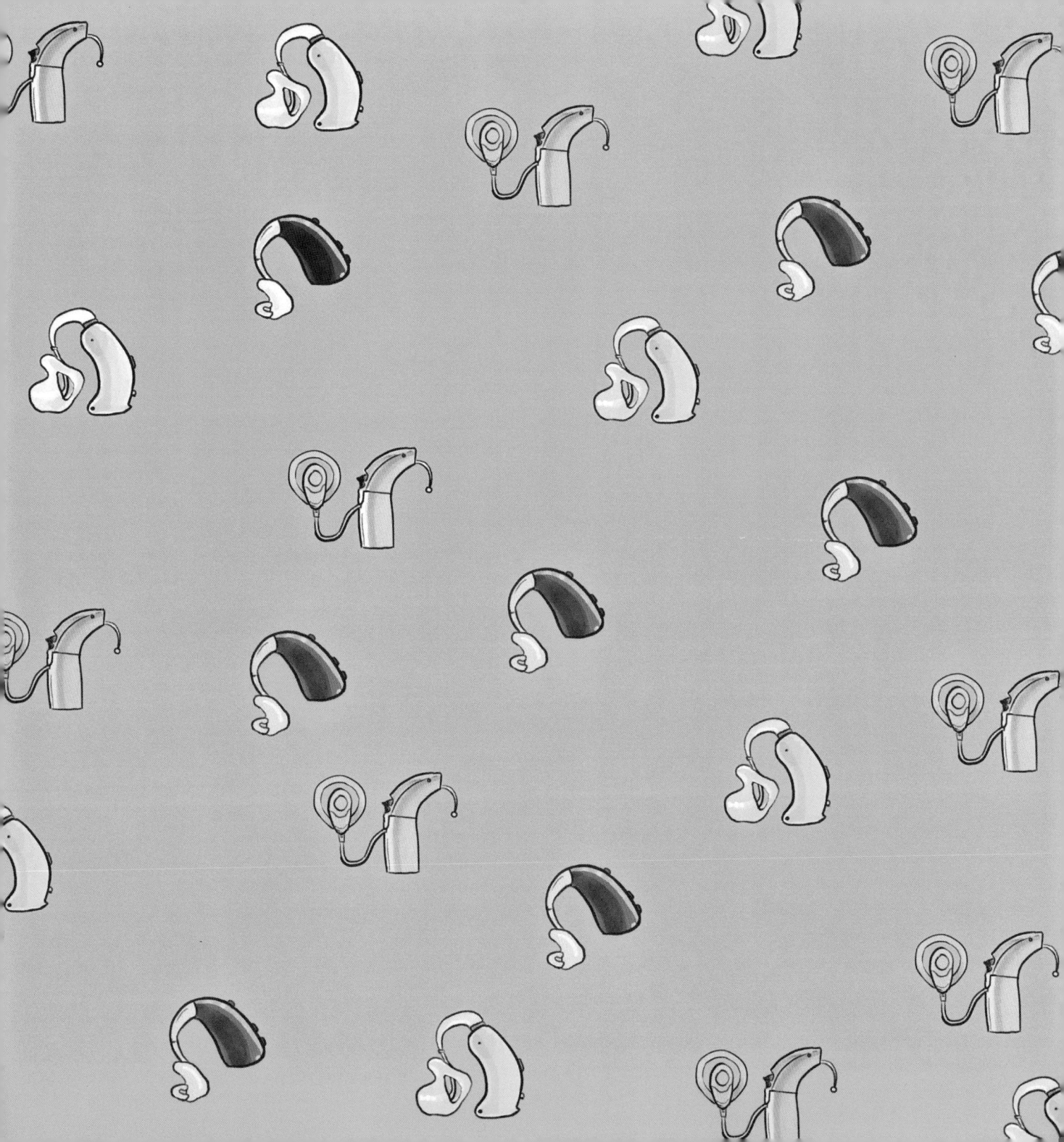

Contributors
    E.R
    M.S

Copyright © 2023 by R. M. Rayner

www.rmrayner.co.uk
https://www.facebook.com/AuthorR.M.Rayner
https://www.instagram.com/r.m.rayner/

All rights reserved.

This book or any portion thereof may not be reproduced or used in any manner whatsoever without the express written permission of the publisher except for the use of brief quotations in a book review.

First printing. 2023

ISBN 978-1-9168791-0-2

Can You Find The SUPERPOWERS?

Written by R. M. Rayner

Illustrated by Harriet Rodis

I want to dedicate this book to someone special, who helped me to accomplish becoming a published children's author.

I have hearing aids myself, so I wanted to be able to help teach families and children how to communicate with others in my position. I hope to enable readers to become more inclusive towards people with hearing loss and other disabilities.

Learn to embrace your disabilities and others will too.

"Hi, Grandpa... GRANDPA!"

"Oh, hello there Freddie, I didn't hear you."

"Grandpa, what's that in your ear?"

"Oh that, that gives me superpowers to hear!" Said Grandpa as they watched the fishes in the pond.

Oh wow, cool! Can I feed the fish?"

"Look at the time, we have to get you to school. Maybe later Freddie."

There were a few new faces! Freddie saw a girl in a blue dress.

"Hi there!

My name's Freddie. Do you want to go on the swings?"

The girl didn't turn.

"Why is she being horrible?" He thought to himself. Freddie didn't know what was wrong.

Tilly came over to Emily and talked to her. They ran off without Freddie and played on the slide with Sam.

"Maybe she doesn't like me?"
Freddie slumped his shoulders.

"There she goes, playing with them."
He whispered to himself.

"I bet you can't run up the slide!" Said Tilly.

"Yeah, I can!" Replied Sam.

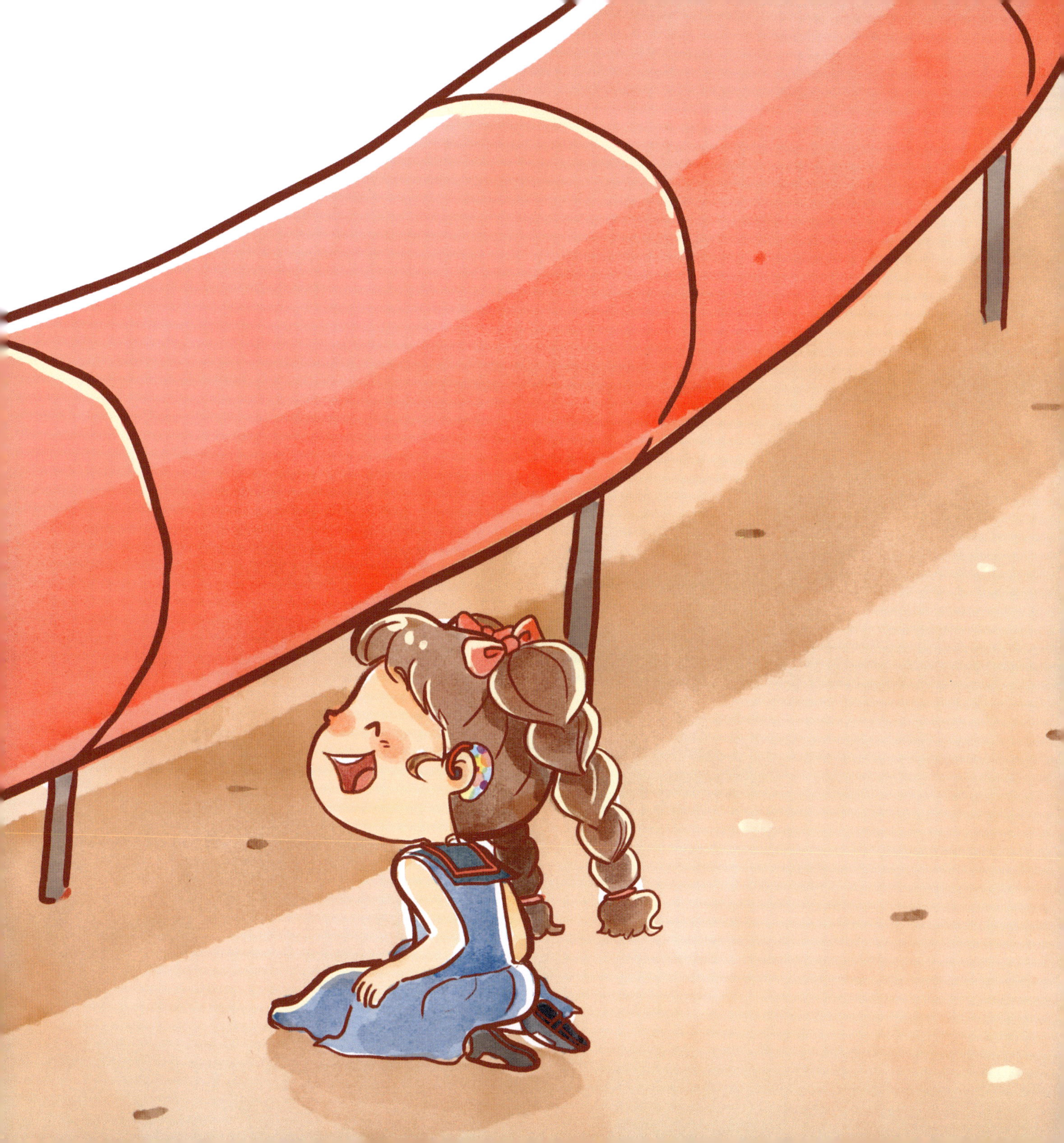

Mrs Redding, Freddie's teacher, knelt down.

"What's wrong, Freddie?"

"That girl in the blue dress ignored me, now they are playing without me!" Freddie said, still crying.

Mrs Redding smiled. "That girl is Emily, she's deaf, which means it gives her

magical powers.

"She needs to **see** you when you **speak**. She **listens** with her **eyes**, so she **watches** your **lips move**.

Either tap her on the shoulder gently or stand in front of her so she sees your face. Does that help?"

"Yes, it does. Thank you, Mrs Redding!" Now it made sense! Emily wasn't mean.

She couldn't hear me when I was talking, just like Grandpa.

"Now you see me!"

Freddie said as he knelt across from Emily.

Emily didn't notice. So, he gently reached out and touched her hand. She looked up, smiling. She watched Freddie's lips as he spoke.

"Hi Emily, my Grandpa has one of those."
Freddie said.

Emily went red from embarrassment.

"I mean, he wears a hearing aid, like you, with

magical powers."

Freddie pointed to his ear.

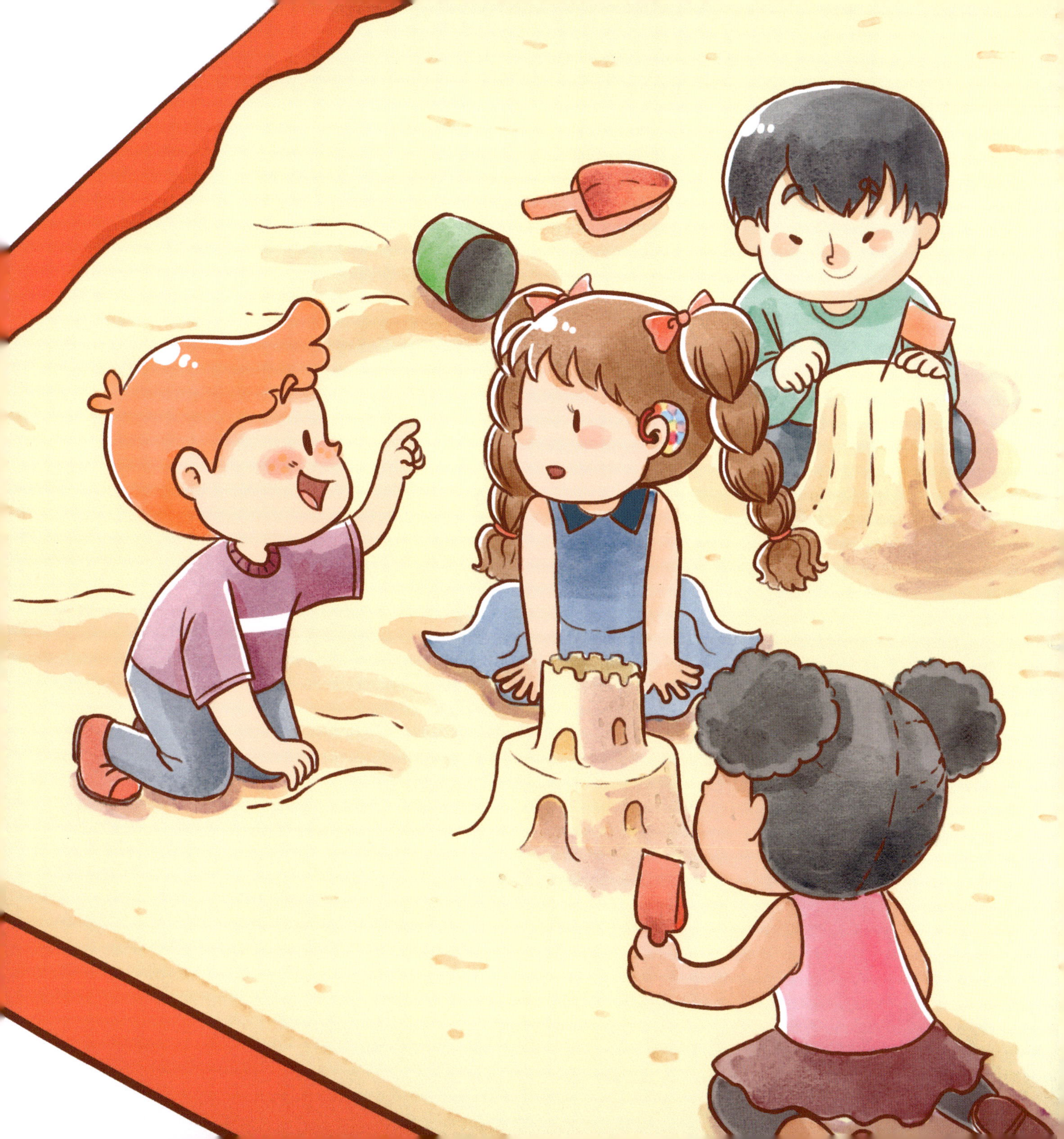

"Oh yeah, it's my

SUPERPOWER.

They help me hear."

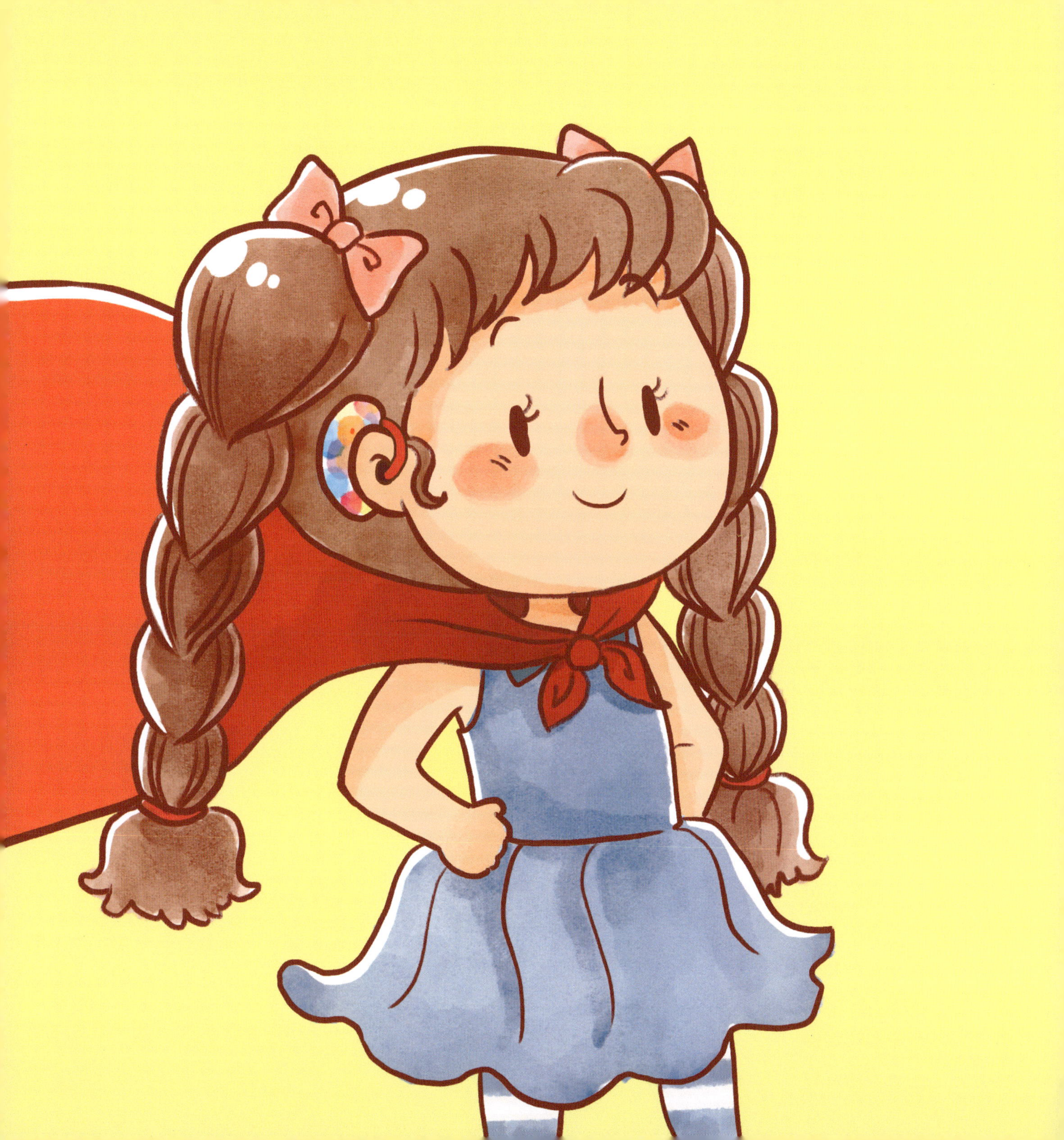

Now Freddie understood Emily was deaf, they were excited to play hide and seek.

Thud! Thud! Thud!

Freddie stomped around like he had the feet of a
giant!

Emily's **eyes grew wide**, she giggled. "Oh no, he's coming...
quick, let's hide!"

The **floor shook** as Freddie's **giant feet** got closer.
From her hiding place behind the slide, Emily looked up.

She giggled when Freddie leaned over the red slide and touched her shoulder gently. Freddie shouted,

"I found you!"

Freddie loved painting. Sam and Tilly joined in.

The children were all laughing together.

Red paint here, blue paint there.

Freddie painted Emily a picture and showed it to her.

There, on the paper, in red, blue and brown paint, were little people playing football.

Emily smiled. "I'll play."

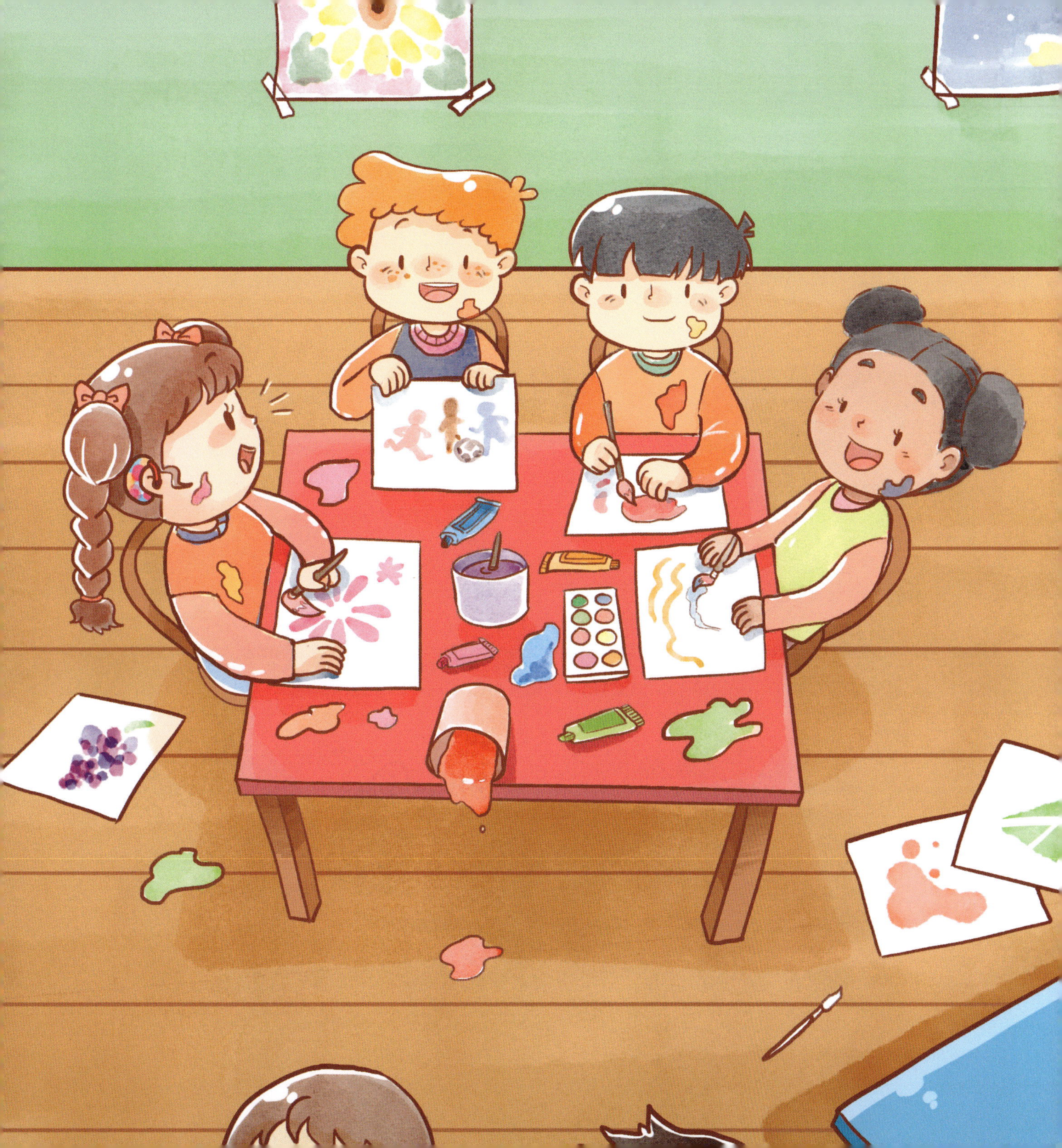

Out on the grassy field, they all played football together.

"Uh oh!" Freddie saw the football flying towards Emily. He ducked down.

He made sure Emily saw him bending down low and covering his head, so Emily copied him!

WHOOOOOOSH

"Wow, that was close!" Emily said in shock.

"Thank you, Freddie," as the football skimmed past the top of her head.

Music time!

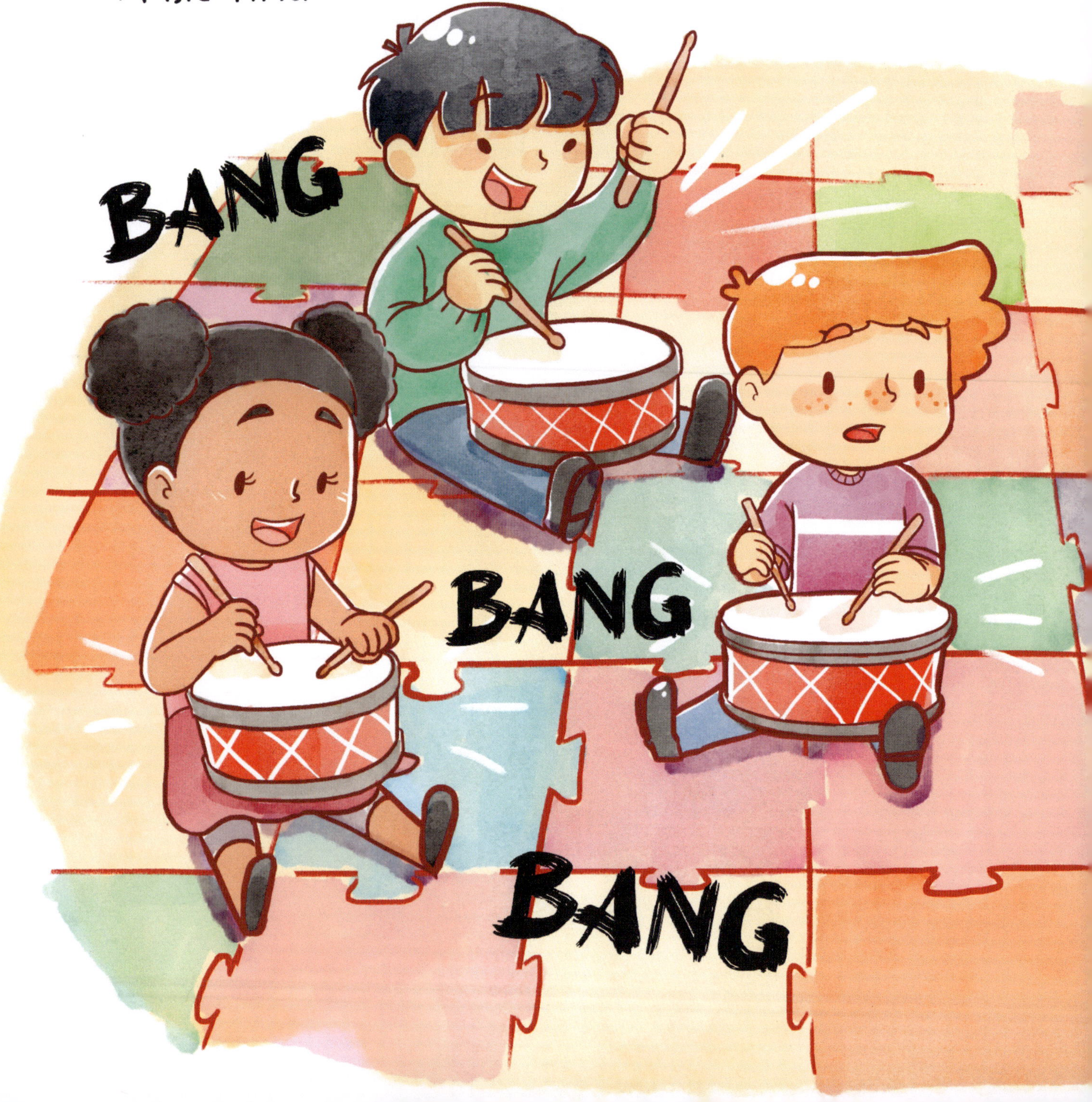

Emily covered her ears.

"Oh, sorry, is it **too loud?**" Said Freddie.

Emily nodded, so Freddie tapped the drums quieter. He said to the others,

"Shhhh, not so loud, please."

Playtime again.

The sky had opened, it was pouring down.

There were lots of puddles.

SPLISH!

SPLASH!

Emily giggled and splashed too.

She pointed to her hearing aid, and Freddie smiled.

"Oh, your magical powers. Can you hear the splashes?"

"Yes, I can with my MAGICAL POWERS."

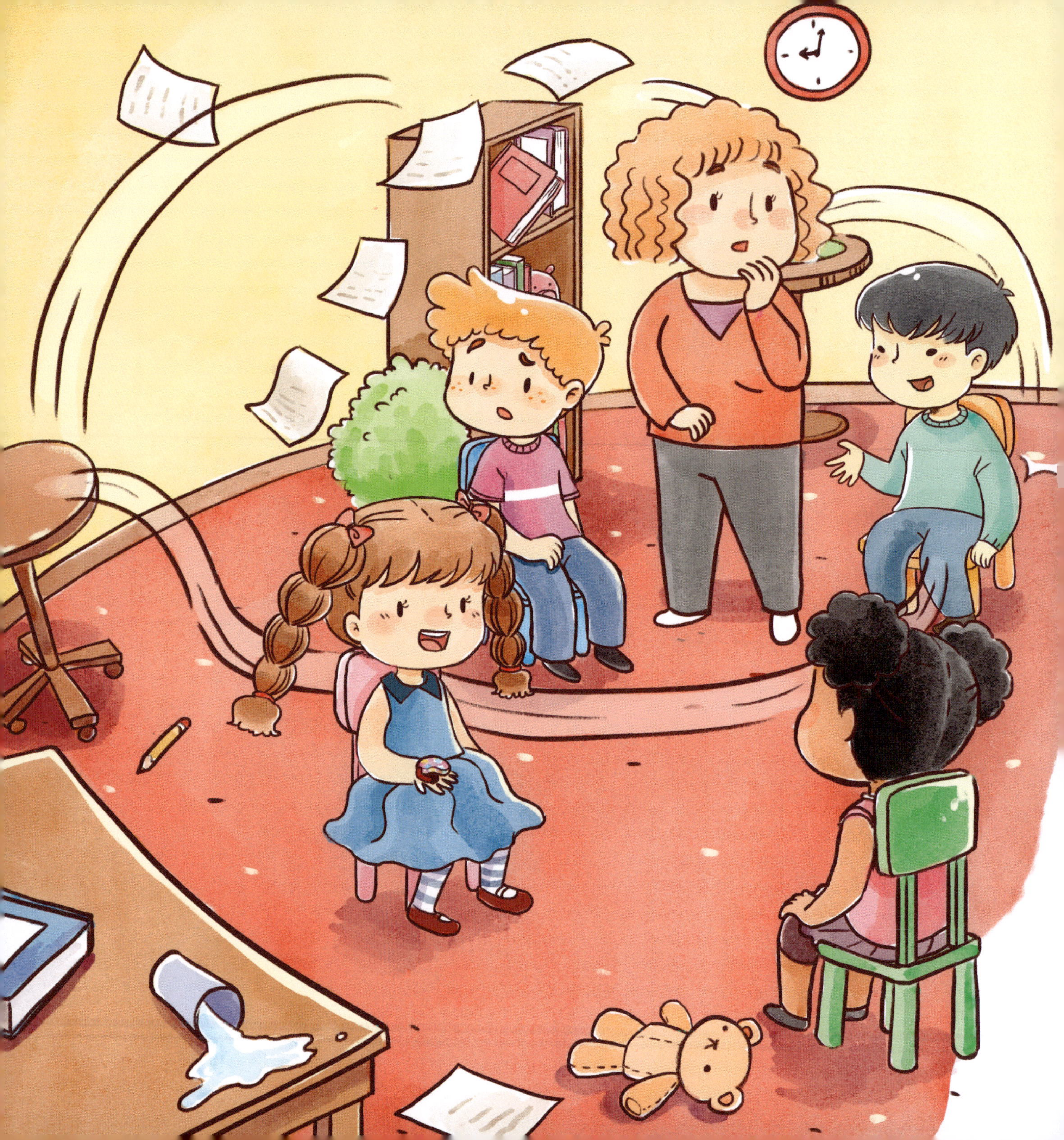

Time for show and tell... Sam says: "This is Patches. He loves to play with his toy mice, and we love to give him warm milk at night."

Loud noises nearby made Emily take out her hearing aid.

Suddenly, Patches leaped out of Sam's arms!

He **pounced** on top of the filing cabinet, then onto **Mrs Redding's desk.** Patches continued bouncing around and even jumped out of the window!

Emily giggled. "Oh, I'm sorry... Patches didn't like the high pitched noise my hearing aid makes, it's a sound only cats can hear. I didn't mean for that to happen."

Was Sam upset? Not at all. He even laughed. "It's okay, Patches is always jumping around at home, too!"

Ring-a-ding-ding!

Yay.

home time.

"Grandpa, my new friend has superpowers like you.

Show him, Emily!"

"It's good to have a secret superpower, isn't it, Emily?"

Emily smiled and giggled.

"See you tomorrow, Freddie!"

"Bye-Bye!"

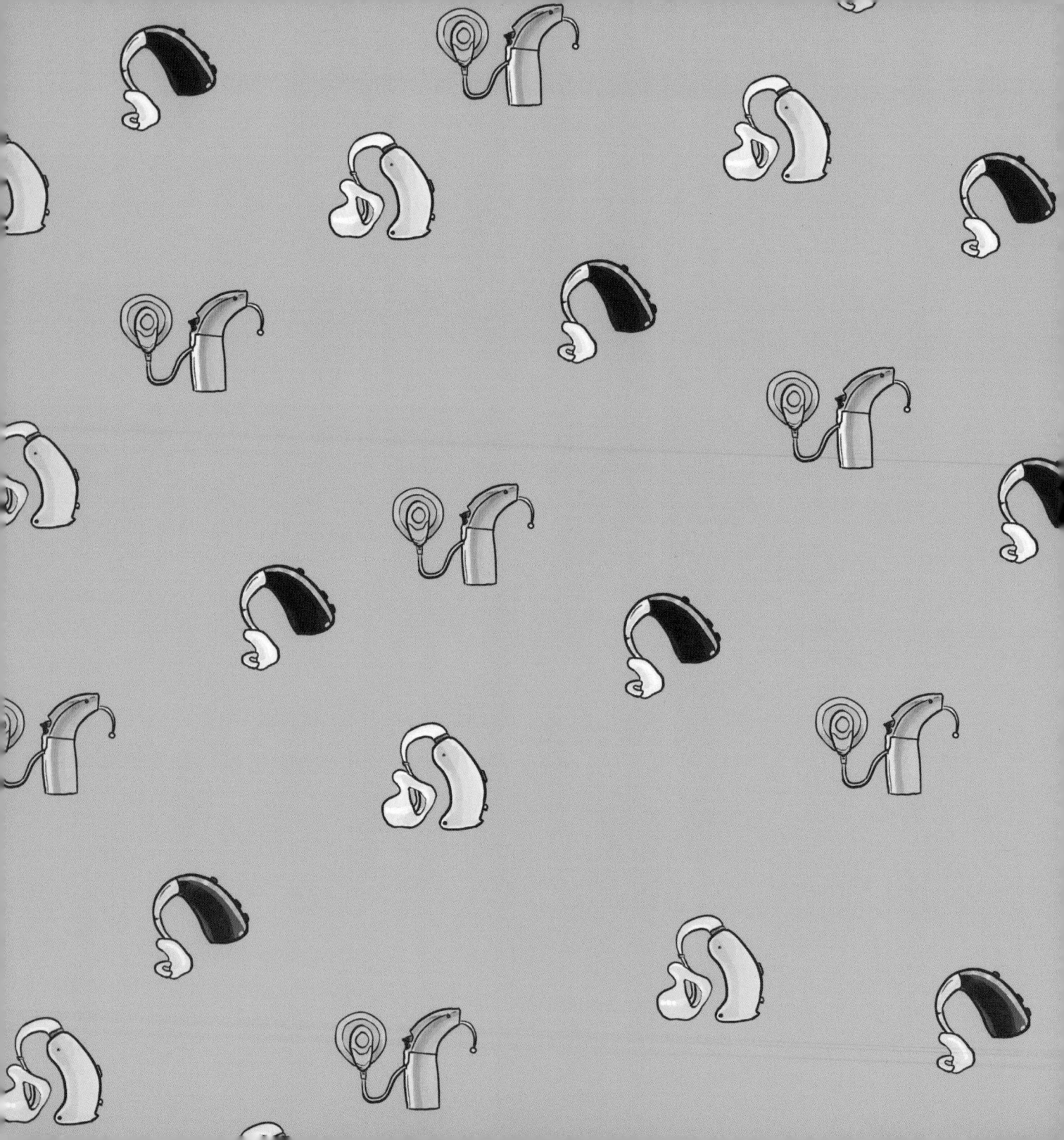

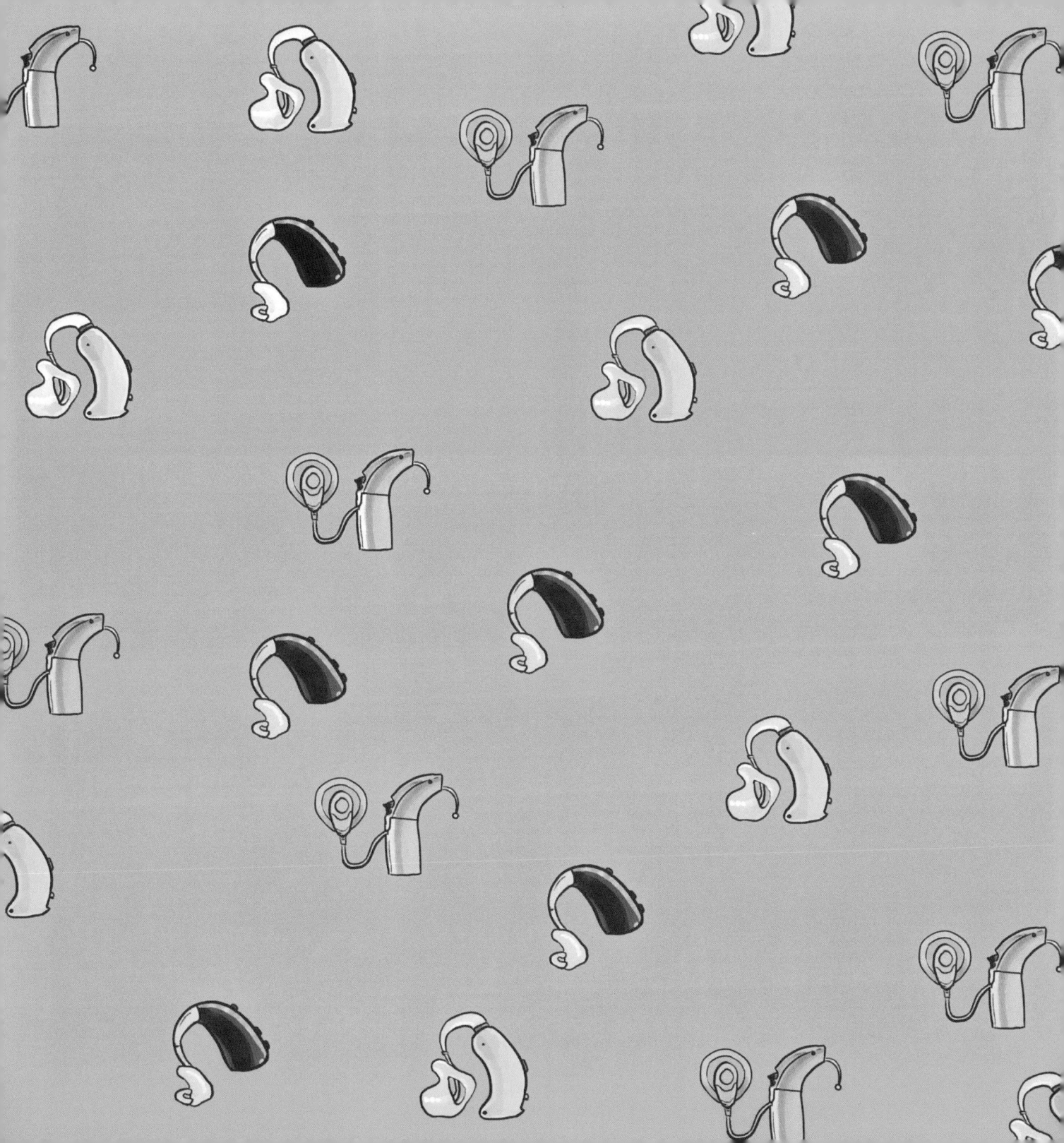

Printed in Great Britain
by Amazon